CRAFT MANIA

36 Fun Crafts for Kids!

- **Paper Cup Mania**

- **Pipe Cleaner Mania**

- **Milk Carton Mania**

Gramercy Books
New York

Previously published in 2002 as three separate volumes under the titles: *Paper Cup Mania*, *Pipe Cleaner Mania*, and *Milk Carton Mania* by Children's Press®, an imprint of Scholastic Inc.

Copyright © 2002 Christine M. Irvin
Photographs © School Tools/Joe Atlas
Design and Production by Function Thru Form Inc.
Illustrations by Mia Gomez, Function Thru Form Inc.

This 2004 edition is published by Gramercy Books, an imprint of Random House Value Publishing, a division of Random House, Inc., New York, by arrangement with Scholastic Library.

Random House
New York • Toronto • London • Sydney • Auckland
www.randomhouse.com

Printed and bound in Singapore

A catalog record for this title is available from the Library of Congress.

ISBN 0-517-22338-4

10 9 8 7 6 5 4 3 2 1

Table of Contents

Table of Contents

Table of Contents

Welcome to the World of
CRAFT MANIA!

Don't throw away that paper cup! Everyday items, such as cardboard tubes and paper plates can become exciting works of art. You can have fun doing the projects in this book and help save the environment at the same time by recycling these household objects instead of just throwing them away.

You can find ways to reuse many things around your home in craft projects. Bottle caps, buttons, old dried beans, and seeds can become eyes, ears, or a nose for an animal. Instead of buying construction paper, you can use scraps of wrapping paper or even last Sunday's comics to cover your art projects. Save the twist ties from bags of bread or vegetables—they make great legs! These are just a few examples of how you can turn garbage into art. Try to think of other things in your home that can be used in your crafts.

 Did You Know?

- Each person creates about 4 pounds (1.8 kilograms) of garbage per day.

- Each person in the United States uses about 580 pounds (260 kg) of paper every year. Businesses in the United States use enough paper to circle the earth 20 times every day!

- Americans use enough cardboard each year to make a paper bale as big as a football field.

- Americans throw away more than 60 billion food and drink cans (like tin cans and soft drink cans) and 28 billion glass bottles and jars (like those from ketchup and pickles) every year.

That's a lot of trash!

What you will need

It's easy to get started on your craft projects. The crafts in this book require some materials you can find around your home, some basic art supplies, and your imagination.

Buttons, bottle caps, beads, old dried beans, or seeds for decoration

Glue

Tape

Tempera paints

Colored markers

Hole puncher

Construction paper (or newspaper or scraps of wrapping paper)

Felt (or scraps of fabric)

Twist ties (or pipe cleaners)

You might want to keep your craft materials in a box so that they will be ready any time you want to start a craft project. Now that you know what you need, look through the book and pick a project to try. Become a Craft Maniac!

A Note to Grown-Ups

Older children will be able to do most of the projects by themselves. Younger ones will need more adult supervision. All of them will enjoy making the items and playing with their finished creations. The directions for most of the crafts in this book require the use of scissors. Do not allow young children to use scissors without adult supervision.

Paper Cup
MANIA

☞ Helpful Hints

Small bathroom cups are good for these projects since they usually do not have the wax coating found on the larger cups. Tacky glue will help construction paper and other materials stick to the cups better than regular white glue.

Ancient Pyramid

What you need

- Ten paper cups, all the same size
- Tape
- Glue

What you do

1. Make the base for your pyramid. Arrange six of the cups in a triangle shape, as shown. Use pieces of tape to hold the cups together at the top where they touch each other, as shown.

2 Make the middle layer of your pyramid. Arrange three of the paper cups in a triangle shape like you did in Step 1. Tape them together at the top the same way you did in Step 1.

3 Put your pyramid together. Carefully, turn the six-cup base of your pyramid upside-down. Spread a layer of glue around the rims of the three-cup layer. Turn them upside-down and press them in place on the six-cup base, in the middle, as shown.

4 Spread a layer of glue around the rim of the last cup. Turn it upside-down and press it in place in the middle of the three-cup layer, as shown. Let the glue dry.

Other Ideas

Add texture to your pyramid. Spread a layer of glue around the sides of your pyramid. Sprinkle sand onto the glue. Let the glue dry completely. Then, tap the loose sand off the paper.

15

Action Figures

- One large paper cup for each figure
- Pencil
- Ruler
- Scissors (Before cutting any material, please ask an adult for help.)
- Construction paper
- Glue
- Markers
- Small buttons, feathers, or pieces of ribbons

What you do

1 Give your action figure some legs. Draw two V shapes, each about 2 inches long, on the rim of the cup with the pencil, as shown. The V shapes need to be the same size and they need to be on opposite sides of the cup. Have an adult help you cut out the V shapes.

2 Create clothing for your figure. Have an adult help you cut out strips of construction paper. You can use one thick strip of construction paper to make a uniform or two thinner strips to make different-colored pants or skirts and shirts. Make sure each strip of paper is long enough to overlap slightly when you wrap it around the cup. Glue the strip or strips to the cup about 1 inch from the bottom of the cup. Let the glue dry. Trim excess paper from V-shaped openings.

3 Add a head. Turn the cup upside-down. Have an adult help you cut out a strip of construction paper that is 1¾ inch wide, as shown. Make sure the strip of paper is long enough to overlap slightly when you wrap it around the cup. Glue the strip of paper to the cup, about 1 inch down, as shown. Let the glue dry.

4 Give your figure a face. Using the markers, draw eyes, a nose, and a mouth on the strip of construction paper.

5 Add details to the clothing. Glue a piece of ribbon around the middle of your action figure for a belt. Glue two small buttons in place for a shirt. Add other small decorative items to finish the uniform the way you want it. Let the glue dry before playing with your action figure.

Other Ideas

- Use beads, seeds, and scraps of fabric or yarn to decorate your figure's head. Cut out a piece of fabric for the mouth. Glue on yarn for hair and beads or seeds for the eyes and nose.

- Make soldiers instead of action figures. For Navy soldiers, cover the cups in white construction paper. Add belts, buttons, and scarves made from blue construction paper, beads, or scraps of fabric.

Cup Catch Game

What you need

- One large paper cup
- Stick (for a handle)
- Scissors (Before cutting any material, please ask an adult for help.)
- Masking tape
- One 15-inch piece of heavy string
- One ½-inch wooden bead
- Pen

What you do

1. Turn the cup upside-down. Poke a hole in the center of the bottom of the cup with a ball-point pen. Place the stick in the center of the hole.

2 Put a handle on your cup. Wrap several layers of masking tape around the stick, about 1 inch from the end. Push the cup down onto the stick, as shown. Keep pushing until the bottom of the cup touches the masking tape. There should be enough tape wrapped around the stick to keep the cup from falling down over the stick. If the cup still falls over the stick, remove the cup, wrap some more tape around the stick, and try again.

3 Tape one end of the string to the end of the stick inside the cup. Wrap the tape around the stick several times to firmly attach the string.

4 Spread glue around the top edge of the tape. Glue the tape to the hole in the cup. Let the glue dry before going on to Step 5.

5 Thread the other end of the string through the bead. Tie the string into a knot around the bead.

Now you're ready to play the cup catch game. The object of the game is to catch the bead in the cup. This can be tricky. Just keep practicing and have fun with it!

Other Ideas

- Use different sizes of cups and beads to make the game more challenging.

- Decorate your cup. Glue different shapes made from construction paper to the outside of the cup.

Ghoulish Ghost

What you need

- One paper cup
- One white facial tissue or a piece of thin white fabric
- Cotton balls
- Glue
- Markers

What you do

1. Attach cotton balls to paper cup. Turn the paper cup upside-down. Spread a layer of glue around the closed end and sides of the cup. Place several cotton balls in the glue, as shown. Let the glue dry before going on to Step 2.

2 Cover the cup with a facial tissue. Put drops of glue on the cotton balls and the sides of the cup. Place the facial tissue over the top of the cup, as shown. Press the tissue on the top and sides of the cup, making sure to smooth out wrinkles. Let the glue dry.

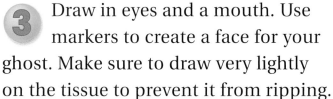

3 Draw in eyes and a mouth. Use markers to create a face for your ghost. Make sure to draw very lightly on the tissue to prevent it from ripping.

That's it!

Other Ideas

- Use small seeds or beads for a face instead of markers.

- Use newspaper or used wrapping paper to make monsters instead of ghosts.

Telephone Time

What you need

- Two paper cups, the same size
- Pen
- Several feet of lightweight string

What you do

1 Turn the cups upside-down. Using a ballpoint pen, have an adult help you punch holes in the center of the bottom of each cup, as shown.

22

2 Put your telephone together. Thread one end of the string up through the hole in one of the cups. Tie a knot in the end of the string. The knot needs to be big enough so that it can't fit back down through the hole. Then, do the same thing with the other end of the string and the other cup. The cups will be joined together by the string, as shown.

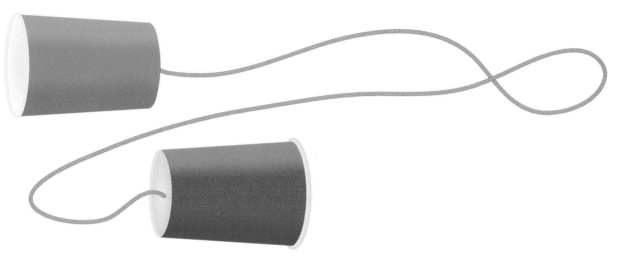

That's it! Your telephone is ready to use. Hold one of the cups up to your mouth, and have a friend hold the other cup up to his or her ear. Make sure that the string is tight. Then talk softly into your cup. Your friend will be able to hear you talking through his or her cup. Take turns talking to each other on your new phone line!

Other Ideas

- Use plastic cups for your telephone instead of paper cups.

- Experiment with different lengths of string to see how far apart you and your friend can talk on your telephone.

Radical Robot

What you need

- One paper cup
- Aluminum foil
- Glue
- Two small buttons (for eyes)
- Small scraps of colored paper or felt (for nose and mouth)
- Twist ties or pipe cleaners (for arms and antennae)
- Scissors (Before cutting any material, please ask an adult for help.)
- Construction paper

What you do

1 Wrap the cup in aluminum foil. Measure a piece of aluminum foil big enough to cover one paper cup from top to bottom. Have an adult help you cut the foil. Then, wrap the foil around the cup, as shown. Fold down the edges of the foil at the top and bottom of the cup to hold it in place.

2 Give your robot a head. Turn the paper cup upside-down. Spread a thick layer of glue on the bottom of it. Crumple a piece of aluminum foil into a ball. Press the foil ball into the glue, as shown. Let the glue dry before going on to Step 3.

3 Give your robot a face. Glue the buttons in place on the head for eyes. Have an adult help you cut shapes from the paper or felt for a nose and mouth. Glue them in place on the robot's face. Let the glue dry before going on to Step 4.

4 Add the antennae and the arms. Glue two twist ties to the paper cup for arms. Bend another twist tie into a V shape and glue it to the top of the head. Let the glue dry before going on to Step 5.

5 Finish your robot. Draw designs on construction paper to decorate the robot's body. Have an adult help you cut out the shapes. Glue the shapes onto the cup. Let the glue dry before playing with your robot.

Other Ideas

Use small metal bolts and washers for the face instead of buttons and fabric.

Make an alien. Cover the cup in green construction paper and use a ball of colored plastic wrap for the head.

25

Magical Mini-Garden

What you need

- Seven paper cups, the same size
- Large polystyrene tray
- Masking tape

- Potting soil
- Pebbles
- Plant seeds

What you do

1. Place the cups on the foam tray with one cup in the center and the other six cups around it. Tape the cups together, as shown.

2 Place pebbles on the bottom of each cup. The pebbles will allow the soil to drain any excess water.

3 Decide what types of plants you want to grow in your mini-garden. Fill the cups about ¾ full with potting soil. Sprinkle a few seeds in each cup. Cover the seeds with a thin layer of potting soil. Sprinkle some water on top of the soil, just enough to make the soil damp.

4 Place the tray in a sunny spot indoors. Water the soil every day until your seeds sprout.

Other Ideas

- Plant flower seeds to make a flower garden.
- Plant herb seeds, such as mint and oregano, to make a kitchen garden.

Speedy Locomotive

What you need

- One bath tissue tube
- Two small boxes, such as empty gelatin boxes
- Glue
- Two small paper cups
- Six large, flat buttons (for wheels)
- Four toothpicks

What you do

1 Spread a layer of glue on one side of one of the gelatin boxes. Press the two gelatin boxes together, as shown, to make a bigger box. Let the glue dry before going on to Step 2.

2 Attach the bath tissue tube to the boxes. Spread a layer of glue around one end of the bath tissue tube. Press the boxes in place on the end of the tube, as shown. Let the glue dry before going on to Step 3.

3 Add a paper cup to the bath tissue tube. Spread a layer of glue around the other end of the tube. Press the paper cup in place over the end of the tube, as shown. Let the glue dry before going on to Step 4.

4 Add a smokestack. Spread a layer of glue around the rim of the other cup. Turn the cup upside-down and glue it to the bath tissue tube, as shown. Let the glue dry before going on to Step 5.

5 Add the wheels. Spread some glue on one of the buttons. Press it in place on the bottom of your locomotive. Glue the other five buttons in place for the other wheels, three wheels on each side. Let the glue dry before going on to Step 6.

6 Connect the wheels. Put a dab of glue on each end of one of the toothpicks. Press the toothpick in place across two of the wheels. Glue another toothpick across the last wheel. Turn the locomotive around and glue the other tooth-picks across the other wheels. Let the glue dry before playing with your locomotive.

Other Ideas

- Paint the bath tissue tube and gelatin boxes with tempera paints.
- Cover the bath tissue tube and the gelatin boxes with construction paper before gluing them together in Step 2.

Wild Windsock

What you need

- One paper cup
- Plastic shopping bag
- Scissors (Before cutting any material, please ask an adult for help.)
- Glue
- Hole puncher
- One 12-inch piece of string

What you do

 Have an adult help you cut the plastic bag into strips about 12 inches long.

2 Spread a layer of glue around the inside of the cup. Press the strips of plastic into the glue, as shown. Let the glue dry before going on to Step 3.

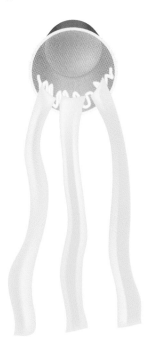

4 Add a hook. Punch two holes in the side of the cup, one on each side. The holes need to be across from each other. Thread one end of the string through one hole and the other end of the string through the other hole, as shown. Tie the two ends of the string, as shown.

3 Have an adult help you cut out the bottom of the paper cup.

5 Hang your windsock in a windy place.

Other Ideas

- Use a plastic cup instead of a paper cup. The plastic cup will last longer outside than a paper cup.

- Decorate your windsock for the seasons. Use flowers for spring, bright colors for summer, leaves for fall, and snowflakes for winter.

Colorful Kaleidoscope

What you need

- One small paper plate
- Pencil
- Scissors (Before cutting any material, please ask an adult for help.)
- Glue
- Scraps of colored plastic wrap or cellophane
- One large paper cup
- Pen

What you do

1 Using the pencil, draw a circle in the center of the paper plate. Have an adult help you cut out the circle, as shown.

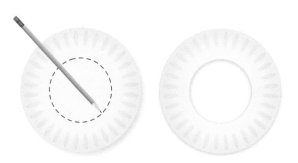

32

2 Glue scraps of colored plastic wrap over the hole you cut out of the paper plate. Let the glue dry before going on to Step 3.

3 Using a ballpoint pen, have an adult help you punch a hole in the bottom of the cup.

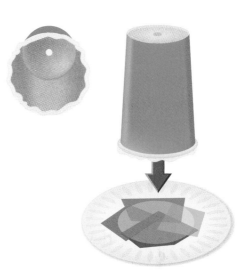

4 Put your kaleidoscope together. Spread a layer of glue around the rim of the paper cup. Press the paper plate in place on the paper cup, as shown. Let the glue dry before playing with your kaleidoscope.

Hold the bottom of the paper cup up to your eye. Look through the hole in the bottom of the cup as you turn the cup to make the colors change.

Other Ideas

○ Decorate the outside of your kaleidoscope. Cover the cup with white construction paper and use markers or crayons to make interesting designs.

Clara the Chicken

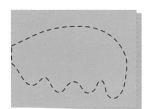

What you need

- **One paper cup**
- **Construction paper** (for the comb, wings, tail, and beak)
- **Pencil**
- **Scissors** (Before cutting any material, please ask an adult for help.)
- **Glue**
- **Two small buttons** (for eyes)

What you do

1 Make the wings. Have an adult help you cut a rectangle from a piece of construction paper. Fold the rectangle in half. Starting at the fold, draw a wing shape. With the paper still folded, cut out the wing shape. Then cut the wing at the fold, as shown. This gives you two even-sized wings.

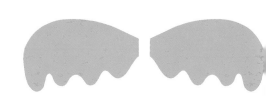

2 Make a comb and a tail for your chicken's body. Draw a comb shape on the paper with the pencil, as shown. For the tail, trace a rectangle on the paper. Have an adult help you cut out these two shapes.

3 Make a beak. Have an adult help you cut out a diamond shape from the construction paper.

4 Add wings to the cup. Fold under the straight edge on the end of the wings about ¼ inch. Spread a thin layer of glue on the folded edge of the wing. Turn the cup upside-down and glue the wings in place, one on each side of the chicken's body, as shown.

5 Add the chicken's comb. Fold under the straight edge of the comb about ¼ inch. Spread a thin layer of glue on the folded edge of the comb. Glue the comb in place on top of the chicken's head.

6 Add the tail. Fold the tail like you are going to make a fan, as shown. Pinch one end of the fan and fold under the paper about ¼ inch. Glue the pinched part of the tail in place on the back of the chicken's body. Hold until the tail begins to stick to the cup.

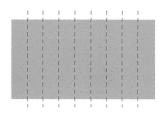

7 Give your chicken a face. Fold the diamond shape in half. Glue the beak in place, as shown. Glue the two buttons in place for eyes. Let the glue dry before playing with your chicken.

Other Ideas

- Make a family of chickens using different sized cups.

Wonderful Windmill

What you need

- Small paper plate
- Pencil
- Scissors (Before cutting any material, please ask an adult for help.)
- Hole puncher
- Plastic straw
- Paper fastener
- One large paper cup
- Glue
- Pen

What you do

1 Make the blades. Using the pencil, draw windmill blade shapes on the paper plate, as shown. Have an adult help you cut out the blade shapes.

36

2 Punch a hole in the middle of the paper plate. Use the hole puncher to make a hole in the end of the straw. Push the end of the paper fastener through the hole in the blades and then through the hole in the straw, as shown. Fasten the ends of the paper fastener loosely so the blades will turn on the straw.

3 Using a ballpoint pen, have an adult help you poke a hole in the bottom of the paper cup. Turn the cup upside-down. Spread a layer of glue around the hole.

4 Push the end of the straw down through the hole in the cup, as shown. Hold the straw in place until the glue sets. Let the glue dry before playing with your windmill.

Other Ideas

Make your windmill with a polystyrene plate and a plastic cup and use it for an outside garden decoration.

Pipe Cleaner MANIA

☞ Helpful Hints

Cutting pipe cleaners can be tricky so make sure to get help from an adult. If a pipe cleaner will not stay twisted together, use a drop of glue to help hold it closed. Tacky glue works better than regular white glue when gluing pipe cleaners.

Wacky Headband

What you need

- **Brown paper shopping bag opened to lie flat**
- **Scissors** (Before cutting any material, please ask an adult for help.)
- **Pencil**
- **Two pipe cleaners**
- **Two cotton balls** (or two buttons)
- **Glue**
- **Ruler**

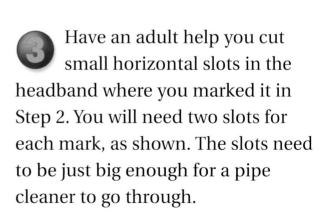

What you do

1 Make the headband. Have an adult help you cut a 2-inch wide strip from the shopping bag big enough to fit around the top of your head, with about ½ inch extra.

2 Use the pencil to mark the headband where you want the antennae attached.

3 Have an adult help you cut small horizontal slots in the headband where you marked it in Step 2. You will need two slots for each mark, as shown. The slots need to be just big enough for a pipe cleaner to go through.

4 Make the antennae. Glue one cotton ball to the end of one pipe cleaner. Do the same with the other cotton ball and pipe cleaner. Let the glue dry before going on to Step 5.

5 Add the antennae. Slide one pipe cleaner end through one of the slots on one side of the headband and out through the other, as shown. Add a drop of glue in the slot to hold the antenna in place. Do the same with the other antenna. Let the glue dry before going on to Step 6.

6 Finish your headband. Wrap the headband around your head. Overlap the ends so it fits snugly on your head. Mark with a pencil where you want the headband to end. Take the headband off and put a drop of glue on one side of the headband. Press the two sides of the headband together. Let the glue dry before wearing your headband.

Other Ideas

- Add glitter to the cotton balls to make them sparkle. Put a drop of glue on each cotton ball. Sprinkle glitter onto the glue. When the glue dries, gently tap off the loose glitter.

- Decorate your headband with markers, paints, glitter, or sequins before adding the antennae in Step 5.

- Use pieces of wallpaper for the headband.

Pencil Toppers

What you need

- One large pipe cleaner
- One small pipe cleaner
- Pencil

What you do

1 Make the head of your pencil topper. Bend the large pipe cleaner to make a loop in the middle, as shown. This is your pencil topper's head.

2 Make the body and legs. Twist the ends of the pipe cleaner together to make the body. Leave a section of both ends of the pipe cleaner untwisted for the legs.

3 Add the arms. Twist the small pipe cleaner once around the pencil topper's body to make the arms, as shown.

4 Hook your pencil topper to a pencil. Bend one arm and one leg over the sides of a pencil.

Other Ideas

○ Give your pencil topper a face. Cut a piece of felt to fit the head section. Glue the felt to the back of the head. Use a felt-tipped marker to draw in eyes, a nose, and a mouth.

○ Make multicolored pencil toppers for different occasions. For instance, a red and white one could be used for Valentine's Day. A brown and orange one could be for fall, Halloween, or Thanksgiving. And a green and white one could be used for either spring or St. Patrick's Day.

Bead Bunny

What you do

1 Make the bunny's body. Thread the beads on both of the pipe cleaners in order from the smallest to the largest, as shown. Leave a larger amount of the pipe cleaners sticking out of the bottom bead for legs. The smallest bead will be the head and the larger beads will be the body.

46

2 Make the ears. Bend the pipe cleaners at the top to make ear shapes, as shown. Put a drop of glue on the top bead to hold the ears in place.

3 Make the feet. Bend the pipe cleaners at the bottom to make feet shapes, as shown. Put a drop of glue on the bottom bead to hold the feet in place.

4 Finish your bunny. Use the marker to draw a face on the top bead. Glue a piece of a cotton ball on the back of the bottom bead for a tail. Let the glue dry before playing with your bunny.

Other Ideas

- Glue a bit of cotton on your bunny's face for the nose.
- Glue two tiny beads on your bunny's face for eyes.
- Paint the beads before putting them together in Step 1. Make sure the paint is completely dry before threading the beads onto the pipe cleaners.
- Use different kinds of beads to make an assortment of bunnies.

47

Silly Glasses

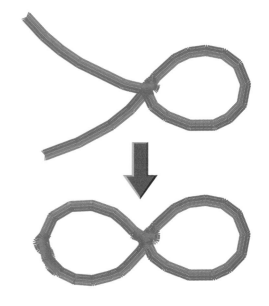

What you need

- **Three pipe cleaners**
- **Scissors** (Before cutting any material, please ask an adult for help.)

What you do

1 Make the lenses section. Fold a pipe cleaner in half. Make a loop using half of the pipe cleaner, as shown. Twist one end of the pipe cleaner around the other to close the first loop. Make another loop with the remaining amount of pipe cleaner. Twist the ends together to close the second loop, as shown.

2 Make the sides of the glasses. Bend each of the other two pipe cleaners to make side frames, each with a hook on the end, as shown. The hook part will fit over your ear.

3 Put your glasses together. Twist the straight end of one side piece around one side of the lenses section, as shown. Do the same with the other side piece.

4 Try on your glasses. Bend each side piece to fit around your ears. If there is excess pipe cleaner material, take the glasses off and have an adult help you cut off any excess.

Other Ideas

Add lenses to your glasses. Wrap the eyeholes with clear or colored plastic wrap.

Flashy Rings

What you need

- **Two pipe cleaners, cut in half, for each ring**
- **One bead or button for each ring**
- **Scissors** (Before cutting any material, please ask an adult for help.)

What you do

1 Twist two pipe cleaners around each other, as shown.

2 Make a ring shape. Bend the pipe cleaners around your finger. Do not twist the ends together.

3 Add some decoration. Thread a bead or a button onto the pipe cleaner.

4 Finish your ring. Twist the ends of the pipe cleaner together, as shown. Have an adult help you cut off any excess pipe cleaner material.

That's it! Your ring is ready to wear.

Other Ideas

- Make an assortment of rings using different colors of pipe cleaners and different beads and buttons.

- Make bracelets instead of rings. You will need one pipe cleaner, uncut, for each bracelet. Bend the pipe cleaner into a circle shape, big enough to fit around your wrist, with a little left over. Add beads or buttons to the pipe cleaner for decorations. Bend both ends of the pipe cleaner to make hooks. Slide the bracelet onto your wrist and hook the ends together.

Pretty Daisy

What you need

- **Two long white pipe cleaners**
- **One yellow pipe cleaner**
- **One long green pipe cleaner**
- **Scissors** (Before cutting any materials, please ask an adult for help.)

What you do

1 Make the center of your daisy. Have an adult help you cut the yellow pipe cleaner in half. Bend one half of the yellow pipe cleaner into a circle. Twist the ends together to close the circle, as shown.

2 Add the petals. Twist one end of one of the white pipe cleaners around the yellow pipe cleaner circle. Bend the white pipe cleaner into a small loop. Wrap it around the circle, as shown, to make the first petal. Continue adding petals until

52

you reach the end of the white pipe cleaner. End with a full loop petal. Wrap the second white pipe cleaner around the circle and continue making petals until you have petals all around the circle.

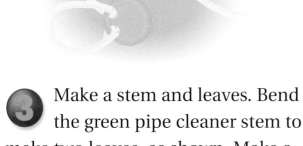

3 Make a stem and leaves. Bend the green pipe cleaner stem to make two leaves, as shown. Make a loop where you want a leaf on the stem. Then wrap the pipe cleaner around the base of the loop. Make a second loop where you want your second leaf. Wrap the pipe cleaner around the base of the second loop.

4 Attach the daisy's head section to the stem section. Twist the top of the stem pipe cleaner once or twice around the edge of the yellow pipe cleaner to hold it in place.

Other Ideas

Make Brown-Eyed Susans. Use a short brown pipe cleaner for the center of the flower and long orange pipe cleaners for the petals.

Make your daisy into a refrigerator magnet. Skip Steps 3 and 4. Instead, have an adult help you cut a piece of a white paper bag to fit the flower center. Glue the paper in place on the back of the flower's center. Then glue a magnet to the back of the paper. Let the glue dry before you stick your flower head magnet to the refrigerator.

Make a daisy hair barrette. Skip Steps 3 and 4. Instead, have an adult help you cut a piece of a white paper bag to fit the flower center. Glue the paper in place on the back of the flower's center. Glue the daisy head to a hair barrette. Let the glue dry before wearing your barrette.

Ring Toss Game

What you need

- One pipe cleaner for each ring
- Several plastic bottles (such as empty soda bottles) to use as targets
- Small pebbles, seeds, or beans

What you do

1 Make rings. Bend each pipe cleaner to make a circle. Twist the ends of the pipe cleaner to hold the circle together, as shown.

Add small pebbles, seeds, or beans to the bottles to weigh them down.

 Set up several bottles on the floor.

That's it! Now you're ready to play the Ring Toss Game. Stand back a few steps from the bottles. Throw a ring and try to make it fall over the neck of a bottle. Score one point for each ring you get on one of the bottles.

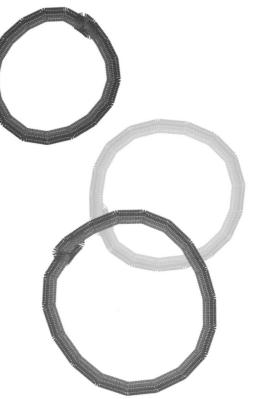

Other Ideas

- Make different sizes of rings using different sizes of pipe cleaners.

- Experiment with different sizes of rings and bottles. Is it easier to ring a small-necked bottle with a small ring or a large one? What about a bottle with a big neck?

Buzzy the Bumblebee

What you need

- Three black pipe cleaners
- One yellow pipe cleaner
- One bead, for the head, big enough to thread on a pipe cleaner
- Glue
- Pencil
- Marker

What you do

1 Give your bumblebee a head. Thread one end of a black pipe cleaner through the bead. Bend the end of the pipe cleaner over so it will not fit back through the hole in the bead. Put a drop of glue on the end of the pipe cleaner to hold the bead in place.

2 Make the wings. Using a black pipe cleaner, bring both ends to the center of the pipe cleaner, making a loop. Twist one end around the center of the pipe cleaner and then twist the other end around the center.

3 Add the wings. Place the pipe cleaner with the bead between the two loops of the other black pipe cleaner. Wrap one of the loops around the pipe cleaner with the bead to secure the wings, as shown.

4 Make the body. Twist the last black pipe cleaner and the yellow pipe cleaner together to make one thick, two-colored pipe cleaner. Then, wrap the two-colored pipe cleaner around the pencil, as shown. Slide the pipe cleaners off the pencil.

5 Put your bumblebee together. Thread the end of the beaded pipe cleaner through the twisted

two-colored pipe cleaners, as shown. Bend the single black pipe cleaner back slightly to connect the body and head sections.

6 Add the face. Draw in eyes and a mouth with the marker.

Other Ideas

- Use tiny beads for the eyes.
- For wider bumblebee body, try wrapping the yellow and black pipe cleaners around a handful of pencils or a thick marker.
- Make your bumblebee into a lapel pin. Glue a large safety pin to the back of your bumblebee. Let the glue dry before wearing your bumblebee lapel pin.
- Make your bumblebee into a magnet. Glue a magnet to the back of your bumblebee. Let the glue dry. Stick your bumblebee magnet to the refrigerator.

57

Fun Mini-Sculptures

What you need

- Two large pipe cleaners for each sculpture
- One large, flat button with two holes
- One small cotton ball or a piece of cotton
- Glue
- Two small beads (for eyes)
- Fabric scraps
- Scissors (Before cutting any material, please ask an adult for help.)
- One bottle cap

What you do

1. Make the head and arms of your sculpture. Bend a pipe cleaner in the middle to make a loop for the head. Twist part of the pipe cleaner together to make the neck. Then, bend both ends of the pipe cleaner to make arms, as shown.

58

2 Add legs to your sculpture. Thread one end of the other pipe cleaner up through one hole in the button and then down through the other hole. Hook both ends of the pipe cleaner legs to the head and arms section. Then, twist the top of the leg section together to hold the arms in place and make the body, as shown.

3 Add a face. Glue a cotton ball to the front of the head section of your sculpture. Then, glue the beads in place on the cotton for eyes.

4 Finish your sculpture. Using the scissors, have an adult help you cut clothes shapes from the fabric scraps, as shown. Glue the clothes in place on your sculpture.

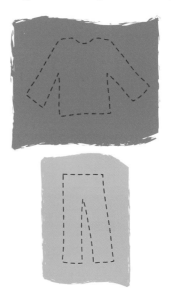

5 Make a stand. Glue the button to the inside of the bottle cap. Let the glue dry before playing with your sculpture.

Other Ideas

- Make your sculptures multicultural by dressing them in ethnic outfits. Try making Japanese kimonos, Mexican serapes, or Indian saris.

- Try making animals instead of people. See if you can make a tiger, a bear, or a flamingo.

Little Mouse

What you need

- One pipe cleaner
- Pencil
- Piece of newspaper (for the ears)
- Scissors (Before cutting any material, please ask an adult for help.)
- Glue
- Cotton ball (for the head)
- Three tiny seeds (for eyes and nose)
- Two small pieces of thread (for whiskers)

What you do

1 Make the body. Twist the pipe cleaner around the pencil, as shown. Leave about 2 inches of the pipe cleaner straight. Slide the pipe cleaner off the pencil.

2 Add the head. Glue the cotton ball head to the end of the body section, as shown. Let the glue dry before going on to Step 3.

3 Add the ears. Have an adult help you cut two small ear shapes from the newspaper, as shown. Glue the ear shapes to the head.

4 Make the tail. Bend the end of the pipe cleaner to make it curved, as shown.

5 Add the face. Glue two seeds in place on the mouse's head for the eyes. Glue the two pieces of thread in place on the head for the whiskers. Glue the last seed in the middle of the whiskers for the nose. Let the glue dry before playing with your mouse.

Other Ideas

- Make your mouse into a lapel pin. Glue a large safety pin to one side of your mouse's body. Let the glue dry before wearing your lapel pin.

- Make your mouse into a refrigerator magnet. Glue a magnet to one side of your mouse's body. Let the glue dry before sticking your mouse to the refrigerator or other magnetic surface.

Walking Stick Insect

What you need

- **Four long pipe cleaners**
- **One small bead** (for the head)
- **Scissors** (Before cutting any material, please ask an adult for help.)
- **Marker**

What you do

1 Make the body. Thread the bead onto the end of one of the pipe cleaners. Bend the end of the pipe cleaner back against the bead just enough to keep the bead from sliding off the pipe cleaner.

2 Make the legs. Have an adult help you cut two pipe cleaners in half. Three pieces will be used for legs. One piece will be used for the antennae.

3 Add the antennae. Take one piece of pipe cleaner and put it under the pipe cleaner body just behind the bead. Make sure that there is an even amount of the pipe cleaner on each side. Then wrap the pipe cleaner piece around the body, as shown.

4 Shape the legs. Take one half of a pipe cleaner and make it into a V shape. Then bend each end of the pipe cleaner into a small circle, as shown. You can use your fingers to mold the circles.

5 Add the legs. Put the first set of legs slightly behind the antennae. Add the pipe cleaner with the point up over the pipe cleaner body. Wrap the pipe cleaner around the body. Add the second set of legs about halfway from the end of the body and wrap the pipe cleaner legs around the body. Add the last set of legs at the end of the body and wrap it around the body, as shown.

6 Add the last pipe cleaner. Twist one end of the pipe cleaner in front of the first set of legs. Then wrap the other end of pipe cleaner around the end of the body. Have an adult help you cut off any excess pipe cleaner.

7 Add a face. Use the marker to make eyes and a mouth on the bead.

Other Ideas

- Make a spider. Make four legs instead of three, and make them all the same size. Skip Step 3. Twist the legs in place on the spider's body without leaving any spaces between them. After you put on the last leg, have an adult help you cut off the end of the body pipe cleaner so it is only about ½ inch long. Bend the end of the pipe cleaner back over the last leg.

- Make a scorpion. Make four legs instead of three, and make them all the same size. Add pincers in Step 3 instead of antennae.

63

Family Tree

What you need

- One stick for the tree trunk
- Pipe cleaners for the branches
- Lump of modeling clay
- Lid from a large spray can
- Construction paper
- Scissors (Before cutting any material, please ask an adult for help.)
- Twist ties
- Hole puncher

What you do

1. Make a tree. Twist pipe cleaners around the stick to make branches, as shown. Make three sets of branches.

2 Put your tree in a pot. Fill the spray can lid with modeling clay. Push the end of the stick all the way down into the clay.

3 Make the leaves. Have an adult help you cut leaf shapes from the colored paper, as shown. You will need one leaf for each member of your family—yourself, your parents, your brothers and sisters, and your grandparents. Write the name of a family member on each leaf.

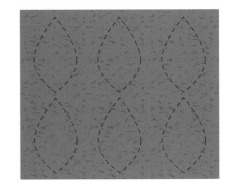

4 Add the leaves. Make a hole in one leaf with the hole puncher. Thread a twist tie through the hole. Wrap the twist tie around one of the branches, as shown. Repeat this process with each of the remaining leaves. Place your grandparents on the upper branches, your parents on the middle branches, and you and your brothers and sisters on the lower ones.

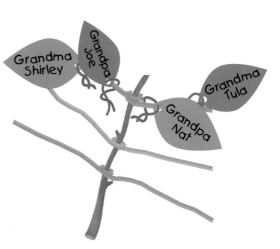

Other Ideas

- Glue small photos of family members to the branches instead of making paper or felt leaves. Have an adult help you cut the photos into leaf shapes, if you like.

- Add smaller branches to your tree by wrapping short pieces of pipe cleaner around the long pipe cleaner branches.

Milk Carton MANIA

☞ Helpful Hints

Remember to rinse out the cartons and let them dry before beginning any project. Poking holes in milk cartons can be challenging so make sure to ask a grown-up for help if you have trouble. When gluing items onto milk cartons, it helps to use big rubber bands to hold things in place while the project dries. Bag clips or big binder clips can be used to keep a milk carton closed while waiting for the glue to dry.

Quick-and-Easy Building Blocks

What you need

- Two milk cartons, the same size, for each building block

- Scissors (Before cutting any material, please ask an adult for help.)

What you do

1 Have an adult help you cut the tops off both milk cartons.

2 Put one milk carton inside the other milk carton to make a solid block. Slide the open end of one carton inside the open end of the other carton, as shown. Squash the top of one carton a little to make it fit inside the other. Push the cartons together until one is completely inside the other.

Your building block is ready to use!

Other Ideas

- Paint your block with tempera paints. Make sure the paint is completely dry before using the block.

- Wrap your blocks in brown paper from an old grocery bag.

- Build with these blocks. They make great forts and cool castles.

Perky Penguin

What you need

- One milk carton, any size
- One large white paper shopping bag, opened up to lie flat, or white construction paper
- Ruler
- Pencil
- Scissors (Before cutting any material, please ask an adult for help.)
- Glue
- Two big, black buttons
- Scrap of red felt
- Black yarn
- Scraps of black felt

What you do

1 Open up the top of the milk carton.

2 Cover the milk carton with the paper. Measure and mark the shopping bag so that it is big enough to cover the open carton from top to bottom, and around all four sides, with an extra ½-inch overlap all around. Have an adult help you cut the white paper. Spread a thin layer of glue around the whole carton. Apply paper to the carton. Use a small amount of glue to hold overlaps in place on the side and bottom.

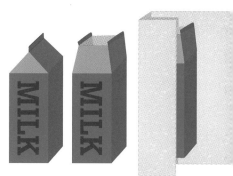

3 Close the carton top and glue shut.

4 Add eyes. Glue on the buttons for eyes.

5 Make the beak. Using the red felt, have an adult help you cut out a diamond shape for the beak, as shown. Fold the felt shape in half. Glue it in place on the penguin's face.

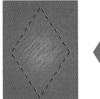

6 Add feathers. Glue scraps of black yarn to the top of the penguin's head. Let the glue dry.

7 Add the wings. Using black felt, have an adult help you cut out two wing shapes, as shown. The wings should be long enough to go from the top to the bottom of the penguin's body. Then, glue the wings in place. Let the glue dry.

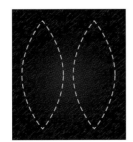

8 Add the feet. Using black felt, have an adult help you cut out two feet shapes, as shown. Glue the feet in place on the bottom of the penguin's body. Let the glue dry.

Other Ideas

Paint your penguin instead of covering the milk carton with paper.

Make a pair of bookends by making two penguins. Before you close the tops of the milk cartons in Step 3, fill each carton halfway with sand.

Space Shuttle

What you need

- One half-gallon milk carton
- One large white paper shopping bag, opened up to lie flat, or white construction paper
- Ruler
- Black marker
- Scissors (Before cutting any material, please ask an adult for help.)
- Glue
- Two soup cans or frozen orange juice cans
- Aluminum foil
- Four small, empty thread spools, all the same size or one cardboard tube cut into four 1½-inch sections

What you do

1. Open up the top of the milk carton.

2. Cover the milk carton. Measure and mark the white bag so that it is big enough to cover the open carton from top to bottom, and around all four sides, with an extra ½-inch overlap all around. Have an adult help you cut the paper. Spread a thin layer of glue around the whole carton. Apply paper to the carton. Use a small amount of glue to hold overlaps in place on the side and bottom.

3 Close the carton top and glue shut. Let the glue dry.

4 Cover the soup cans. Measure and mark a piece of aluminum foil so that it is big enough to cover one soup can from top to bottom, with an extra ½-inch overlap at the top. You will need a piece of foil about 8 inches by 8 inches. Have an adult help you cut the foil. Then, wrap the foil around the soup can, as shown. Fold down the edges of the foil at the top and bottom of the can to hold it in place. Cover the other soup can the same way.

5 Put your space shuttle together. Turn the soup cans upside-down. Spread a thick layer of glue on one side of one soup can.

Press the soup can in place on one side of the milk carton, as shown. Do the same thing with the other soup can. Let the glue dry.

6 Add exhaust pipes. Glue the four thread spools to the bottom of your space shuttle, as shown. Let the glue dry.

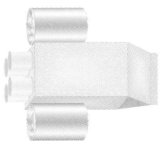

7 Add windows. Using the marker, draw in window shapes on your space shuttle anywhere you want them. Color them in with markers.

Other Ideas

- Decorate your space shuttle with decals left over from model-building projects or with stickers.

- Draw your own signs on your space shuttle with markers.

Carton Cat

What you need

- **One milk carton, any size**
- **One large brown paper bag, opened up to lie flat**
- **Ruler**
- **Black marker**
- **Scissors** (Before cutting any material, please ask an adult for help.)
- **Glue**

- **Scraps of felt**
- **Three buttons**
- **Three twist ties or pipe cleaners**
- **One thick, fuzzy pipe cleaner or a scrap of furry material**
- **One bag clip or large binder clip**

What you do

1 Open up the top of the milk carton.

2 Cover the milk carton with paper. Measure and mark the paper bag so that it is big enough to cover the open carton from top to bottom, and around all four sides, with an extra ½-inch overlap all around. Have an adult help you cut the brown paper. Spread a thin layer of glue around the whole carton. Apply paper to the carton. Use a small amount of glue to hold overlaps in place on the side and bottom.

3 Close the carton top and glue shut. Use a bag clip or large binder clip to hold the carton shut. Let the glue dry before going on to Step 4.

4 Add ears. Draw ear shapes on the felt, as shown. Have an adult help you cut them out. Glue them in place on the milk carton.

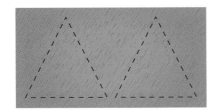

5 Add eyes. Glue the two buttons for eyes and one button for the nose.

6 Add whiskers. Glue the three twist ties on the face for whiskers. Let the glue dry before going on to Step 7.

7 Add the legs. Using the black marker, draw in legs for your cat.

8 Add a tail. Glue the thick, fuzzy pipe cleaner or the

scrap of furry material in place, for the tail, as shown. Let the glue dry before playing with your cat.

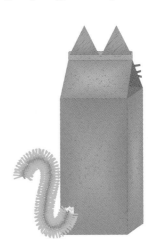

Other Ideas

○ **Paint your cat.** Instead of covering the milk carton with brown paper, paint it with tempera paints, using any colors you wish.

○ **Turn your cat into a doorstop.** Before you close the top of the milk carton in Step 3, fill the carton halfway with sand. This will make the carton heavy enough to hold a door open. Follow the rest of the directions to finish your cat.

Ring The Bell

- **One half-gallon milk carton**
- **Scissors** (Before cutting any material, please ask an adult for help.)
- **Ruler**
- **Markers**
- **Construction paper**
- **Glue**
- **One piece of string, ribbon, or yarn about 18 inches long**
- **Two ½-inch bells**
- **Pen**

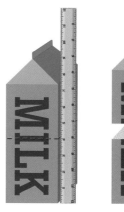

What you do

1 Cut the top part off of a milk carton. Measure and draw a line 4 inches up from the bottom of the carton around all four sides. Have an adult help you cut along the line. The bottom part of the carton will be used for the bell.

2 Cover the bottom piece of the carton. On construction paper, trace around one side of the bell four times. Trace around the top one time. Have an adult help you cut out the pieces of paper. Spread a thin layer of glue on one side of the bell. Press a piece of construction paper onto the bell, keeping edges even. Glue on one piece of paper at a time until all four sides and top of the bell are covered. Let glue dry before going on to Step 3.

3 Add a hole to the carton. With an adult's help, use the pen to punch a hole in the middle of the top of the carton.

4 Make a clapper for the inside of the carton. The clapper is the part of the bell that hits the side and makes it ring. Have an adult help you cut a piece of ribbon or yarn 18 inches long. Fold the string in half and pull the looped end through the opening in the carton so that the string extends 4½ inches above the carton. Tie a knot above the carton and one below. Tie a bell to each end of the string inside the carton.

5 Decorate the carton. Use markers and draw designs on your bell.

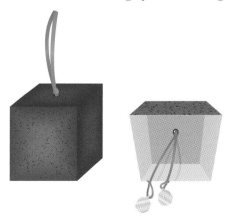

Other Ideas

- Paint your bell with tempera paints. Make sure the paint is completely dry before using the bell.

- Make an assortment of bells, using different sized milk cartons. Use a different sized bell for each clapper, a small one for small bells and larger ones for large bells.

- Cover your bell with wrapping paper for special events, such as birthdays and holidays.

Handy Basket

What you need

- One half-gallon milk carton
- Scissors (Before cutting any material, please ask an adult for help.)
- Glue
- Ruler
- Masking tape
- Pen
- Two paper fasteners
- Tempera paints
- Paintbrush

What you do

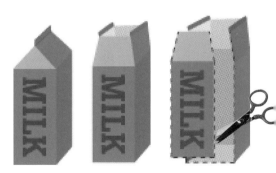

1. Open the top of the milk carton and have an adult help you cut one side off of the milk carton, as shown.

2. Close the end of the milk carton. Fold the remaining top flaps down and glue them together, as shown.

80

3 Make the handle. Measure and mark a 1-inch by 7½-inch piece from the side of the carton that you cut out in Step 1. Have an adult help you cut out the handle. Also, using a pen, punch a hole in each end of the handle, and two holes (one on each of the long sides of the basket) where you want the handles attached.

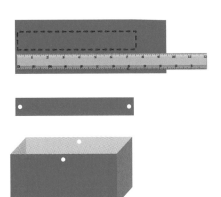

4 Attach the handle to the basket. Line up the holes in the handle with the holes in the basket. Slide a paper fastener through each hole, from the outside to the inside. Open the fasteners to hold the handle in place.

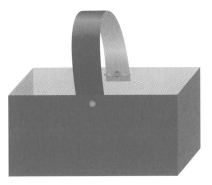

5 Paint your basket with tempera paints. Make sure the paint is completely dry before using your basket.

Other Ideas

Cover the milk carton in construction paper instead of painting it.

Use the basket as a planter. Place some pebbles in the bottom of the basket. Fill the basket with soil and plant a few seeds in the dirt. Water and watch your favorite plants grow.

Use as a gift basket. After decorating your basket, fill it with small presents for a friend or member of your family.

Kooky Clown

What you need

- **One half-gallon milk carton**
- **Glue**
- **Construction paper**
- **Ruler**
- **Scissors** (Before cutting any material, please ask an adult for help.)
- **One egg carton**
- **Two buttons**
- **Markers**
- **Cotton balls or scraps of yarn** (for hair)
- **One bag clip or large binder clip**

What you do

1 Cover the milk carton with construction paper. Measure and mark a piece of construction paper big enough to cover one open carton from top to bottom, and around all four sides, with an extra ½-inch overlap all around. Have an adult help you cut the construction paper. Spread a thin layer of glue around the carton. Apply paper to the carton.

Smooth out wrinkles and overlap at top, bottom, and on each side as you go around. Use a small amount of glue to hold overlaps in place on the sides and bottom.

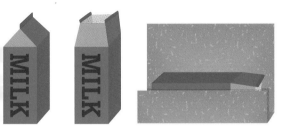

2 Glue the top of the milk carton together so it won't come open. Use a bag clip or large binder clip to hold the carton closed while the glue dries.

3 Have an adult help you cut the bottom half of an egg carton into three parts, as shown, each with two rows of two cups.

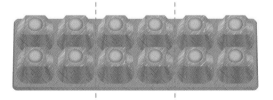

4 Glue one section of the egg carton on the bottom of your carton for legs. Glue one section on each side of the carton for arms.

5 Glue on buttons for eyes.

6 With markers, design a face for your clown.

7 Give your clown some hair by gluing on cotton balls or scraps of yarn. Let the glue dry before playing with your clown.

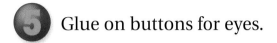

Other Ideas

Decorate your clown's costume with fabric or paper in different designs.

Add hands and shoes made from scraps of cardboard.

Make a clown hat from construction paper or newspaper.

Have a contest with your friends to see who can make the funniest or silliest clowns.

What you need

- One half-gallon milk carton
- One large brown paper bag, opened up to lie flat
- Ruler
- Markers
- Scissors (Before cutting any material, please ask an adult for help.)
- Glue
- One bag clip or large binder clip

What you do

 1 Open up the top of the milk carton.

2 Cover the milk carton. Measure and mark the paper bag so that it is big enough to cover the open carton from top to bottom, and around all four sides, with an extra ½-inch overlap all around. Have an adult help you cut the brown paper. Spread a thin layer of glue around the whole carton. Apply paper to the carton. Use a small amount of glue to hold overlapping pieces in place on the side and bottom.

3 Close the carton top and glue shut. Use a bag clip or large binder clip to hold the carton closed while the glue dries. Let glue dry before going on to Step 4.

4 Cut the carton into two sections. Draw a line around three sides of the milk carton with a marker about 3 inches from the bottom of the carton. Have an adult help you cut along the line. Then, fold the bottom part of the carton up and out. The big part of the carton will be the house and the small part will be the garage.

5 Attach the smaller part of the carton to the larger part. Spread a thick layer of glue on the side of the smaller part that touches the larger part, as shown. Use a bag clip or large binder clip to keep the house

and garage attached until the glue dries. Let the glue dry before going on to Step 6.

6 Add the doors. Using markers, draw a door shape on the house and a door shape on the garage.

7 Add windows. Using markers, draw window shapes on the house and the garage where you want them. Color in the window shapes with a marker.

Other Ideas

- Open the doors using scissors. Ask an adult for help cutting the doors.

- Color your house and garage with crayons.

- Paint your house and garage. Instead of covering the milk carton with brown paper, paint it with tempera paints, using any colors you wish.

- Make a town by building lots of houses.

Crazy Critter

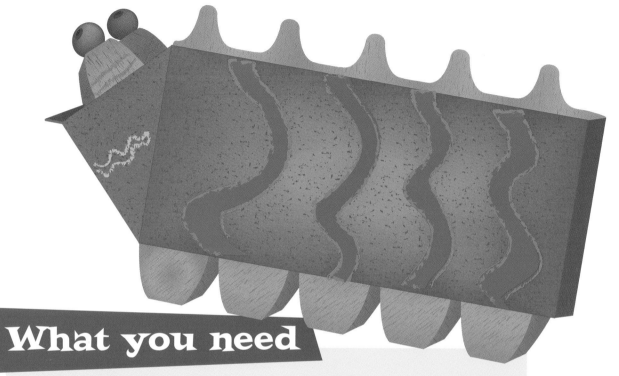

What you need

- **One half-gallon milk carton**
- **One egg carton**
- **Tempera paints**
- **Paintbrush**

- **Glue**
- **Scissors** (Before cutting any material, please ask an adult for help.)

What you do

1. Take the bottom of the egg carton and cut off one row of egg holders, as shown. Have an adult help you cut the carton.

2. Glue the larger section of the egg carton bottom to one side of the milk carton.

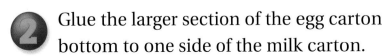

86

With the milk carton on its side, glue the two egg sections to one side of the peak of the carton's top. These two egg holders will be the critter's eyes. If the carton has a plastic spout at the top, glue the egg section to the side opposite the spout.

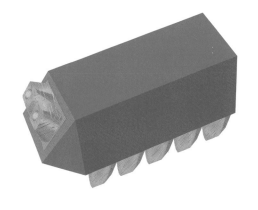

Take the top of the carton and cut off the edges, as shown. Glue the ridges from the top of the egg carton to the top of the milk carton.

After the glue has dried, paint the egg holders and milk carton any colors you would like.

Add eyes and mouth with tempera paints. Let the paint dry before playing with your critter.

Other Ideas

- Use buttons, beads, or seeds for your critter's eyes and mouth.
- Make a rock monster by gluing on pebbles instead of painting your critter.

Bird Feeder

What you need

- One half-gallon milk carton
- Marker
- Scissors (Before cutting any material, please ask an adult for help.)
- Pen
- Two polystyrene plates
- One long piece of thick string
- Stick for perch

What you do

1 Make the square-shaped holes on the carton. Using the marker, draw squares in the front and the back of the carton, as shown. Have an adult help you cut out the shapes.

2 Make a hole in the center of each plate and in the bottom of the milk carton.

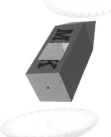

3 Tie a big knot on one end of the string. Pull the string through the hole in one of the plates and then through the hole in the bottom of the milk carton. Open the top of the carton. Pull the string through the top and close the carton.

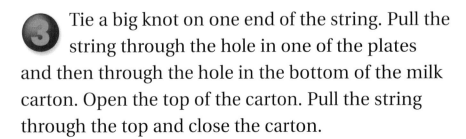

4 Pull the string through the hole in the other plate.

5 Tie the end of the string at the top into a handle.

6 Add the perch. Using the pen, have an adult help you punch two holes in the feeder, one below each square opening. Push one end of the stick in through one hole and out through the other hole, as shown. Make sure the stick hangs out about the same amount on each side of your bird feeder.

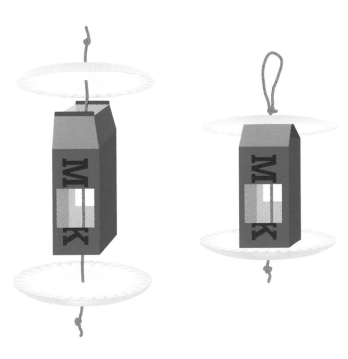

7 Hang your bird feeder from a tree branch where birds can find it and other animals cannot reach it. Fill your feeder with sunflower seeds or other wild bird food.

Other Ideas

- Get a book on birds out of the library and see if you can identify the types of birds that visit your feeder.

- Decorate your bird feeder.

Wishing Well

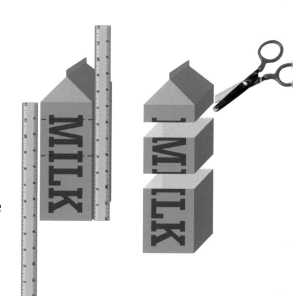

What you need

- **One milk carton, any size**
- **Ruler**
- **Marker**
- **Scissors** (Before cutting any material, please ask an adult for help.)
- **Construction paper**
- **Glue**
- **Four craft sticks**
- **Lightweight cardboard**

What you do

1 Cut the top part off of a milk carton. Draw a line about 1 inch from the top of the carton. Have an adult help you cut off the top of the carton along the line.

2 Make the base for the well. Measure and mark a line 4 inches up from the bottom of the carton around all four sides of the carton.

On a piece of construction paper, trace around one side of the carton base four times. Have an adult help you cut out the pieces of paper. Spread a thin layer of glue on one side of the wishing well. Press a piece of construction paper onto the well, keeping the edges even. Glue one piece of paper at a time until all four sides of the well are covered. Let the glue dry before going on to Step 4.

Lie the base on its side. Glue one craft stick flat against one of the inside corners of the well 1 inch down inside the carton. Let glue dry. Add the remaining craft sticks in each corner one at a time, as shown. Let the glue dry before going on to Step 5.

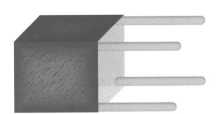

Make a roof for your well. Glue the four craft sticks inside each corner of the carton's top.

Finish the roof. Have an adult help you cut a piece of lightweight cardboard and a piece of construction paper the same size. Both pieces have to be big enough to cover the top of the milk carton. Glue the construction paper to the cardboard. Let the glue dry before going on to Step 7.

Fold the cardboard in half with the construction paper on the outside. Glue the cardboard to the top of the well.

Other Ideas

Use scraps of fabric, wrapping paper, or newspaper to decorate the roof of your well.

Glue pebbles around the base to make a stone well.

Castle Magic

What you need

- **Four milk cartons**
- **One cardboard box,** roughly same height as milk cartons
- **Construction paper**
- **Ruler**
- **Markers**
- **Scissors** (Before cutting any material, please ask an adult for help.)
- **Glue**
- **Toothpicks**
- **Four small beads**

What you do

1 Open up the top of the milk carton.

2 Cover the carton towers. Measure and mark a piece of construction paper big enough to cover one open carton from top to bottom, and around all four sides,

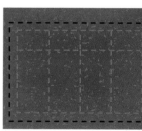
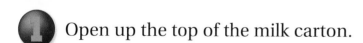

with an extra ½-inch overlap all around. Have an adult help you cut the construction paper. Spread a thin layer of glue around the carton. Apply paper to the carton. Smooth out wrinkles and overlap at top, bottom, and on one side as you go around. Use a small amount of glue to hold overlaps in place on the side and bottom. Repeat the process for all carton towers.

3 Close each carton top and glue shut. Before the glue dries, insert a toothpick into the peak of each milk carton. Let glue dry before going on to Step 4.

4 Cover the cardboard box with construction paper. Make sure to overlap the paper at the top, bottom, and on one side of the box. Let glue dry before going on to Step 5.

5 Glue the carton towers to the outside of the box. Let glue dry before going on to Step 6.

6 Decorate your castle. Use markers to draw windows and a door on the castle towers.

7 Add flags. Glue small pieces of construction paper to toothpicks to make banners. Glue a small bead on the top of each toothpick to cover the end. Let glue dry before playing with your castle.

Other Ideas

Add a drawbridge to the castle. Use a marker to draw an arched doorway in the front of the box, as shown. Have an adult help you cut out the shape (on both sides and the top), leaving the drawbridge attached to the box at the bottom. Fold drawbridge out.

Cover your castle with newspaper or brown paper bags instead of construction paper.

Index

About the Author

Christine M. Irvin lives in the Columbus, Ohio area with her husband, her three children, and her dog. She enjoys writing, reading, doing arts and crafts, and shopping.